PIANO
Adventures®

by Nancy and Randall Faber

THE BASIC PIANO METHOD

FABER
PIANO ADVENTURES®

3042 Creek Drive
Ann Arbor, Michigan 48108

About Piano Adventures® Christmas

The Christmas season is the perfect time to inspire practice at the piano with favorite Christmas melodies.

The playing of carols at the piano enhances many family Christmas traditions and creates meaningful musical memories. Teacher duets are included to promote early-level "chamber music" with a musical family member. Many students enjoy recording the carols (with teacher duet) as a Christmas gift for a parent, relative, or friend.

This book features unique "Sightreading Stocking Stuffers" which are presented with each piece.

Each "stocking stuffer" is a short, carefully written melody which is drawn from the rhythms and intervals in the piece. A student should sightread one "stocking stuffer" a day, and may wish to circle the stocking after playing. These effective sightreading exercises develop the requisites for good reading: intervalic reading, note recognition, and awareness of musical patterns.

A fun-filled Christmas Music Calendar features writing review.

Students may do one per day during the month of December. However, many students find it too tempting to wait, and prefer to complete the calendar earlier in the season.

> **With *Piano Adventures® Christmas,* the teacher can enjoy a carefully conceived pedagogical approach throughout the Christmas season, while the student enjoys treasured holiday music!**

Production: Frank and Gail Hackinson
Production Coordinator: Marilyn Cole
Editors: Victoria McArthur
Cover and Illustrations: Terpstra Design, San Francisco
Engraving: Graybear Music Company, Hollywood, Florida

ISBN 978-1-61677-141-6

CONTENTS

Stuffing the Stockings (theory review) 5

Angels We Have Heard on High 6
  Glorious Stocking Stuffers 7

Carol of the Bells 8
  Caroling Stocking Stuffers 11

Jingle Bell Boogie 12
  Swingin' Stocking Stuffers 15

Bring a Torch, Jeannette, Isabella 16
  Village Stocking Stuffers 18

O Holy Night 19
  Starry Night Stocking Stuffers 22

Dance of the Sugar Plum Fairy 24
  Sugar Plum Stocking Stuffers 26

Jesu, Joy of Man's Desiring 27
  Joyous Stocking Stuffers 30

Christmas Music Calendar 31

About the "Sightreading Stocking Stuffers"

A student's enthusiasm for learning Christmas music can become an opportunity to create enthusiasm for sightreading. In this book, each Christmas song is presented with short melodies, called "Sightreading Stocking Stuffers."

The "Sightreading Stocking Stuffers" are **melodic variations** of the carol being studied. Through repetition of familiar rhythmic and melodic patterns, the student begins to build a visual and aural musical vocabulary.

The "stocking stuffers" provide opportunity for transposition, reinforcing theory and musicianship skills.

The student should sightread one "stocking stuffer" a day while learning the Christmas song. Or, the stocking stuffers can be used as sightreading during the lesson itself.

The teacher may wish to tell the student:

> **Sightreading means "reading music at first sight."**
> When sightreading, music is not practiced over and over. Instead, it is only played several times with the highest concentration.

The following **3 C's** may help the student with sightreading:

CORRECT HAND POSITION
Find the correct starting note for each hand.
Scan the music for rhythmic and melodic patterns.

COUNT - OFF
Set a steady tempo by counting one "free" measure before starting to play.

CONCENTRATE
Focus your eyes on the music, carefully reading the intervals.
Remember to keep your eyes moving ahead!

FF114

Note to Teacher: This page reviews scale steps (scale degrees) in C, G, and F major.
It helps prepare the student for the pieces and sightreading that follow.

Stuffing the Stockings

These "musical gifts" are steps of the major scale: **1 2 3 4 5 6** or **7**.

First name the key signature: C, G, or F major.
Then connect the note in each "gift" to the correct "scale step stocking."

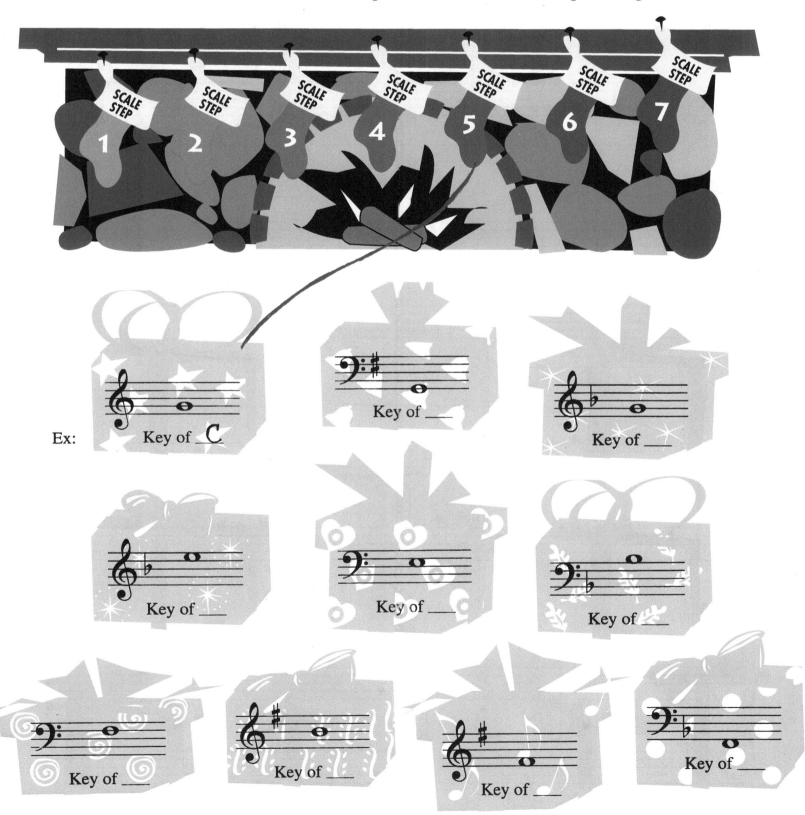

Angels We Have Heard on High

Traditional

FF114

Sightread one "stocking stuffer" a day while learning the carol. Your teacher may also ask you to transpose.

Circle the stocking after sightreading!

GLORIOUS STOCKING STUFFERS

("variations" for sightreading)

Can you transpose to G major?

Can you transpose to D major?

Can you transpose to F major?

Can you transpose to G major?

 DAY 5 Write **I** or **V7** under the Alberti bass for the first stocking stuffer.

 DAY 6 Put a ✔ above each measure of the carol that uses only notes of the C chord. Hint: There are 5.

Carol of the Bells

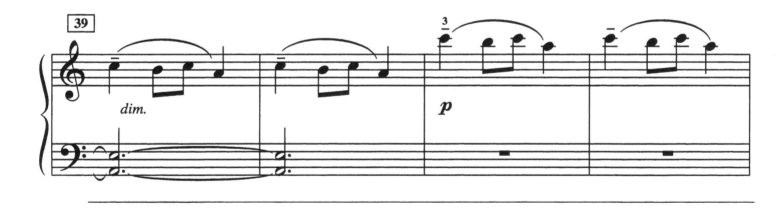

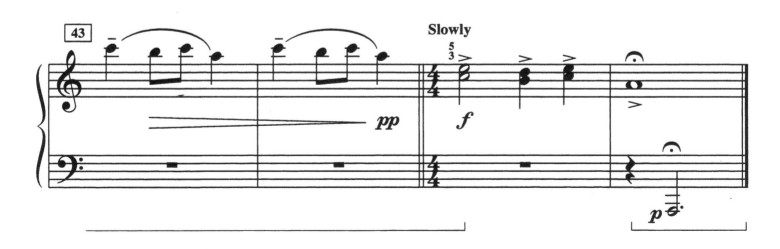

Sightread one "stocking stuffer" a day
while learning *Carol of the Bells*.

Circle the stocking after sightreading!

CAROLING STOCKING STUFFERS

("variations" for sightreading)

Can you transpose to D minor?

Can you transpose to D minor?

Copy the last two measures
of the carol (R.H. only).

Now transpose the last two measures
of the carol to D minor (R.H. only).

Jingle Bell Boogie

Words and Music by
J. Pierpont
(adapted)

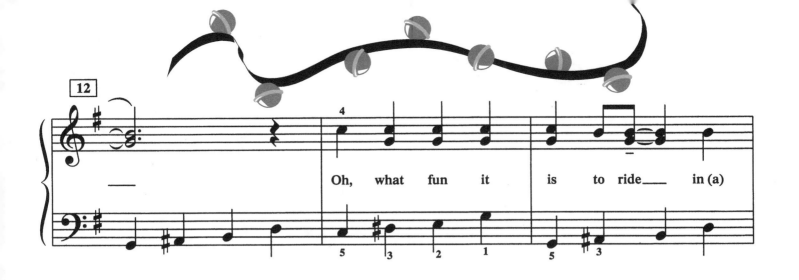

Oh, what fun it is to ride___ in (a) one - horse o - pen...

swing the 8ths!

To Coda ⊕

"Take it away, Santa!"

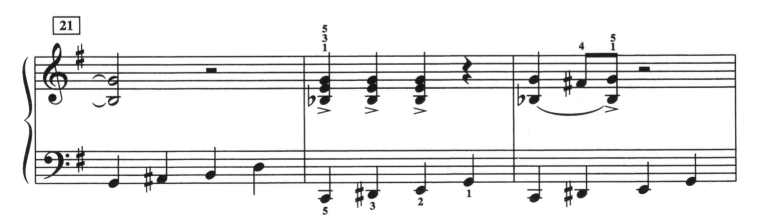

*Note: The 8th notes should be played in a long-short rhythm pattern.
This gives a lilt or **swing** to the music.

D.C. al Coda

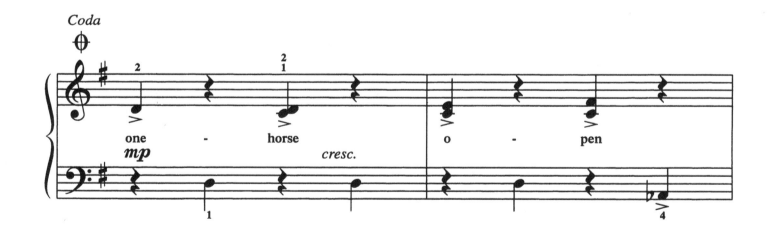

Sightread one "stocking stuffer" a day while learning *Jingle Bell Boogie*.

Circle the stocking after sightreading!

SWINGIN' STOCKING STUFFERS

("variations" for sightreading)

Can you transpose to C major?

DAY 1 — With swing — *mf* — swing the 8ths!

Can you transpose to F major?

DAY 2 — With swing — *f* — *rit.*

DAY 3 — With swing — *f*

Can you transpose to C major?

DAY 4 — With swing — *mf* — swing!

DAY 5 — Name the correct step of the scale for each note below: **1 2 3 4 5 6** or **7**.

scale step *3* __ __ __ __ __
Ex.

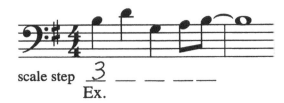

DAY 6 — Name the correct step of the scale for each note below: **1 2 3 4 5 6** or **7**.

scale step *1* __ __ __ __ __
Ex.

Bring a Torch, Jeannette, Isabella

Moderately fast

Traditional

Bring a torch,___ Jean - nette, Is - a -

bel - la! Bring a torch___ come swift - ly and run!

Christ is born, tell the folk of the vil - lage; Je - sus is

16

FF114

sleep - ing   in   his   cra - dle.   Ah,   ah,

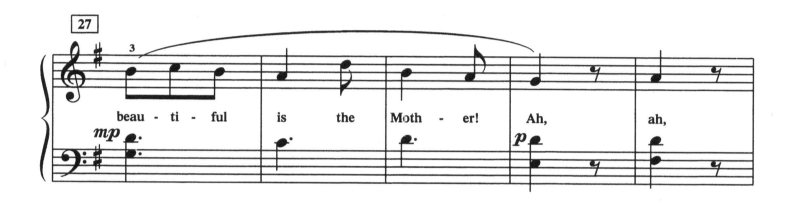

beau - ti - ful   is   the   Moth - er!   Ah,   ah,

beau - ti - ful   is   her   Son!

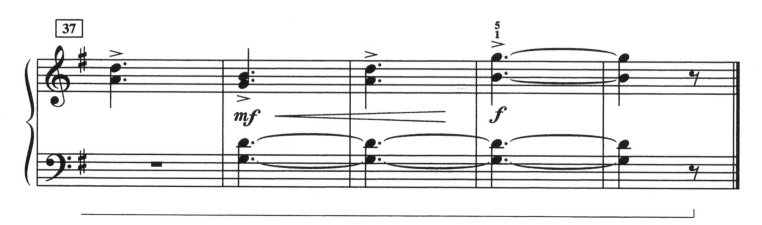

Sightread one "stocking stuffer" a day
while learning *Bring a Torch, Jeannette, Isabella.*

Circle the stocking after sightreading!

("variations" for sightreading)

O Holy Night

Adolph Adam

Moderately

p *mp*

O ho - ly night!_____ The

stars are bright - ly shin - ing. It is the

night of the dear Sav - iour's birth.

Long lay the world_____ in

sin and sor - row pin - ing, till He ap -

Sightread one "stocking stuffer" a day while learning *O Holy Night.*

Circle the stocking after sightreading!

Your teacher may ask you to write **I**, **IV**, or **V7** below each measure before sightreading.

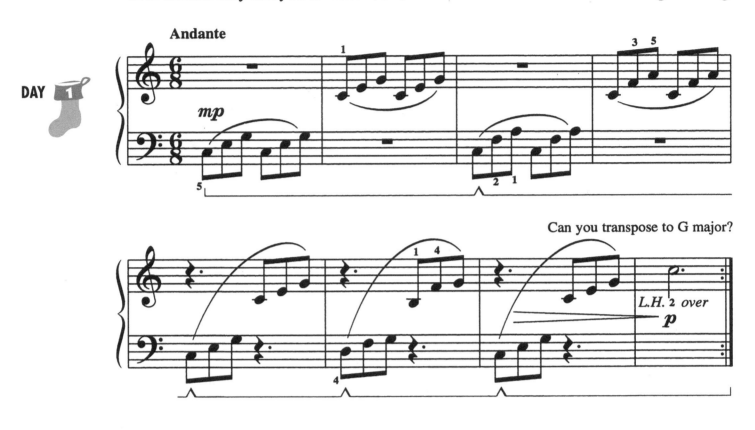

Can you transpose to G major?

Write the counts (1 2 3 4 5 6) for the first two measures before sightreading.

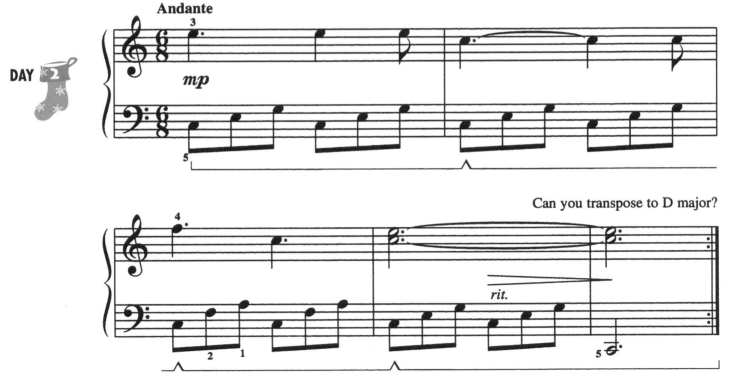

Can you transpose to D major?

FF114

Write the counts (1 2 3 4 5 6) for measures 1- 4 before sightreading.

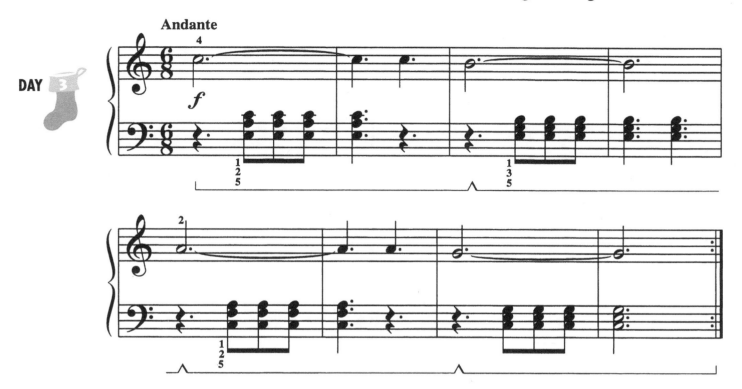

Label the **I** and **V7** broken chords before sightreading.

Can you transpose to F major?

 DAY 5 Write **I**, **IV**, or **V7** below each measure for the first page of *O Holy Night.*

 DAY 6 Write two measures of your own rhythm in ⁶⁄₈ time.

Dance of the Sugar Plum Fairy
(from *The Nutcracker Suite*, Op. 71)

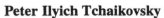

Peter Ilyich Tchaikovsky

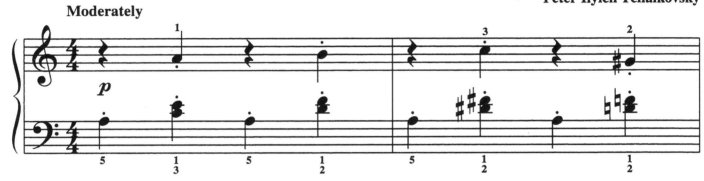

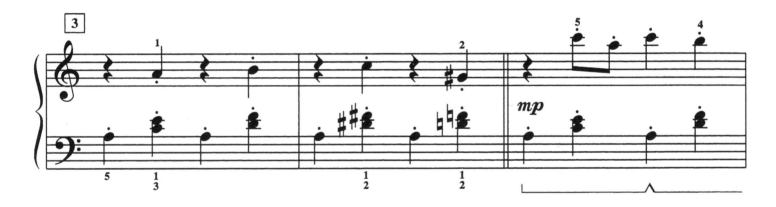

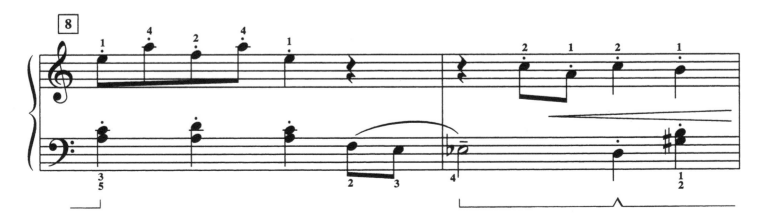

Sightread one "stocking stuffer" a day
while learning *Dance of the Sugar Plum Fairy*.

Circle the stocking after sightreading!

("variations" for sightreading)

Can you transpose to D minor?

DAY 5 In A minor, what is the tonic note? ____ the dominant note? ____

In *Dance of the Sugar Plum Fairy*, circle two places where the L.H. plays the **dominant** moving to the **tonic.**

DAY 6 Where does the music of measures 5-8 appear later in the piece?

measures ____ to ____.

26

Jesu, Joy of Man's Desiring

Johann Sebastian Bach

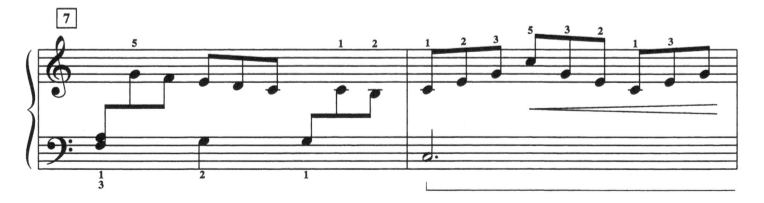

Sightread one "stocking stuffer" a day
while learning *Jesu, Joy of Man's Desiring.*

Circle the stocking after sightreading!

("variations" for sightreading)

Can you transpose to D major?

DAY 1

DAY 2

optional pedal

Can you transpose to G major?

DAY 3

DAY 4

DAY 5

Write a measure of your own
¾ rhythm. Include triplets.

DAY 6

This piece has 3 sections: **section A,
section B,** and a return of **section A.**

Label these sections in your music.

Christmas Music Calendar

Complete the music calendar for each day of December.

DEC. 1 — Name the **key signature**. Key of ____

DEC. 2 — Draw a whole note a **7th above** the star.

DEC. 3 — Draw a whole note a **7th below** the star.

DEC. 4 — Write the **time signature** for these Christmas ornaments.

DEC. 5 — Circle the leading tone in the F scale.
F G A Bb C D E F

DEC. 6 — Write **1 2 3 4** under the correct beats.

DEC. 7 — **C** = $\frac{4}{4}$ — True or False *(circle one)*

DEC. 8 — Draw an **accent mark** below the bell.

DEC. 9 — Draw a **fermata** above the fruitcake.

DEC. 10 — Draw a **tenuto mark** under the note.

DEC. 11 — In $\frac{3}{8}$, the ♩ receives how many beats?
1 2 3 *(circle one)*

DEC. 12 — Draw an **eighth rest** on the tree.

DEC. 13 — Write the **time signature** for this rhythm.

DEC. 14 — In $\frac{6}{8}$, the ♩. receives how many beats?
1 2 3 4 5 6 *(circle one)*

DEC. 15 — Draw a **crescendo sign.**

DEC. 16 — Draw a **diminuendo** sign.

DEC. 17 — Write the dynamic mark for *very soft* sounds.

DEC. 18 — Draw a whole note an octave above the star.

DEC. 19 — Draw a whole note on **ledger line E.**

DEC. 20 — Draw a whole note on **ledger line A.**

DEC. 21 — Circle the correct chord name.
I, IV, or V^7

DEC. 22 — Write the abbreviated word that means to *gradually slow down*.

DEC. 23 — Write 2 measures of your own rhythm in $\frac{3}{8}$ time.

DEC. 24 — **Christmas Eve!** Write two measures of your own rhythm in $\frac{6}{8}$ time.

DEC. 25 — **Christmas Day!** *Play your favorite Christmas pieces!*

F1141

31

Level 3A Supplementary Material by Faber & Faber

Piano Adventures® Popular Repertoire	FF1260	**Discover Blues Improvisation** (with online audio)	FF1155CD
Piano Adventures® Christmas (with "sightreading stocking stuffers")	FF1141	**I Can Read Music, Book 3** (a notespeller)	FF1227
Piano Literature Book 1 (Developing Artist Library - with online audio)	FF1030	**PracticeTime Assignment Notebook**	FF1167
Piano Sonatinas Book 1	FF1110	**Practice & Progress Lesson Notebook**	FF1024

FunTime® Piano Series:

Faber Studio Collection	FF3020
Popular	FF1007
Classics	FF1022
Kids' Songs	FF3004
Favorites	FF1054
Rock 'n Roll	FF1023
Jazz & Blues	FF1010
Ragtime & Marches	FF1008
Hymns	FF1033
Christmas	FF1006

Achievement Skill Sheets:

No. 3 One-Octave Major Scales and Arpeggios	AS5003

Achievement Solo Sheets:

Classic Sonatina in G	A2015
Willow Tree Waltz	A2002